**I0178172**

# FOREWORD

The collection of "Everything Will Be Okay" travel phrasebooks published by T&P Books is designed for people traveling abroad for tourism and business. The phrasebooks contain what matters most - the essentials for basic communication. This is an indispensable set of phrases to "survive" while abroad.

This phrasebook will help you in most cases where you need to ask something, get directions, find out how much something costs, etc. It can also resolve difficult communication situations where gestures just won't help.

This book contains a lot of phrases that have been grouped according to the most relevant topics. You'll also find a mini dictionary with useful words - numbers, time, calendar, colors...

Take "Everything Will Be Okay" phrasebook with you on the road and you'll have an irreplaceable traveling companion who will help you find your way out of any situation and teach you to not fear speaking with foreigners.

# TABLE OF CONTENTS

T&P Books Publishing

T&P Books Publishing

# PHRASEBOOK
# - JAPANESE -

## THE MOST IMPORTANT PHRASES

This phrasebook contains
the most important
phrases and questions
for basic communication
Everything you need
to survive overseas

By Andrey Taranov

T&P BOOKS

Phrasebook + 250-word dictionary

# English-Japanese phrasebook & mini dictionary

By Andrey Taranov

The collection of "Everything Will Be Okay" travel phrasebooks published by T&P Books is designed for people traveling abroad for tourism and business. The phrasebooks contain what matters most - the essentials for basic communication. This is an indispensable set of phrases to "survive" while abroad.

You'll also find a mini dictionary with 250 useful words required for everyday communication - the names of months and days of the week, measurements, family members, and more.

T&P Books Publishing
www.tpbooks.com

ISBN: 978-1-78492-407-2

This book is also available in E-book formats.
Please visit www.tpbooks.com or the major online bookstores.

# PRONUNCIATION

| Hiragana | Katakana | Rōmaji | Japanese example | T&P phonetic alphabet | English example |
|----------|----------|--------|------------------|----------------------|-----------------|

## Consonants

| Hiragana | Katakana | Rōmaji | Japanese example | T&P phonetic alphabet | English example |
|----------|----------|--------|------------------|----------------------|-----------------|
| あ | ア | a | あなた | [a] | shorter than in ask |
| い | イ | i | いす | [i], [iː] | feet, Peter |
| う | ウ | u | うた | [u], [uː] | book, shoe |
| え | エ | e | いいえ | [e] | elm, medal |
| お | オ | o | しお | [ɔ] | bottle, doctor |
| や | ヤ | ya | やすみ | [jɑ] | young, yard |
| ゆ | ユ | yu | ふゆ | [ju] | youth, usually |
| よ | ヨ | yo | ようす | [jɔ] | New York |

## Syllables

| Hiragana | Katakana | Rōmaji | Japanese example | T&P phonetic alphabet | English example |
|----------|----------|--------|------------------|----------------------|-----------------|
| ば | バ | b | ばん | [b] | baby, book |
| ち | チ | ch | ちち | [tʃ] | cheese |
| だ | ダ | d | からだ | [d] | day, doctor |
| ふ | フ | f | ひふ | [f] | face, food |
| が | ガ | g | がっこう | [g] | game, gold |
| は | ハ | h | はは | [h] | home, have |
| じ | ジ | j | じしょ | [dʒ] | joke, general |
| か | カ | k | かぎ | [k] | clock, kiss |
| む | ム | m | さむらい | [m] | magic, milk |
| に | ニ | n | にもつ | [n] | name, normal |
| ぱ | パ | p | パン | [p] | pencil, private |
| ら | ラ | r | いくら | [r] | rice, radio |
| さ | サ | s | あさ | [s] | city, boss |
| し | シ | sh | わたし | [ɕ] | sheep, shop |
| た | タ | t | ふた | [t] | tourist, trip |
| つ | ツ | ts | いくつ | [ts] | cats, tsetse fly |
| わ | ワ | w | わた | [w] | vase, winter |
| ざ | ザ | z | ざっし | [dz] | beads, kids |

# LIST OF ABBREVIATIONS

## English abbreviations

| | | |
|---|---|---|
| ab. | - | about |
| adj | - | adjective |
| adv | - | adverb |
| anim. | - | animate |
| as adj | - | attributive noun used as adjective |
| e.g. | - | for example |
| etc. | - | et cetera |
| fam. | - | familiar |
| fem. | - | feminine |
| form. | - | formal |
| inanim. | - | inanimate |
| masc. | - | masculine |
| math | - | mathematics |
| mil. | - | military |
| n | - | noun |
| pl | - | plural |
| pron. | - | pronoun |
| sb | - | somebody |
| sing. | - | singular |
| sth | - | something |
| v aux | - | auxiliary verb |
| vi | - | intransitive verb |
| vi, vt | - | intransitive, transitive verb |
| vt | - | transitive verb |

# JAPANESE PHRASEBOOK

This section contains
important phrases that may
come in handy in various
real-life situations.
The phrasebook will help
you ask for directions, clarify
a price, buy tickets, and
order food at a restaurant

T&P Books Publishing

# PHRASEBOOK CONTENTS

T&P Books Publishing

## The bare minimum

|  |  |
|---|---|
| Excuse me, ... | すみません、…<br>[sumimasen, ...] |
| Hello. | こんにちは。<br>[konnichiwa] |
| Thank you. | ありがとうございます。<br>[arigatō gozai masu] |
| Good bye. | さようなら。<br>[sayōnara] |
| Yes. | はい。<br>[hai] |
| No. | いいえ。<br>[īe] |
| I don't know. | わかりません。<br>[wakari masen] |
| Where? | Where to? | When? | どこ？ | どこへ？ | いつ？<br>[doko ? | doko e ? | i tsu ?] |

| I need ... | …が必要です<br>[... ga hitsuyō desu] |
| I want ... | したいです<br>[shi tai desu] |
| Do you have ...? | …をお持ちですか？<br>[... wo o mochi desu ka ?] |
| Is there a ... here? | ここには…がありますか？<br>[koko ni wa ... ga ari masu ka ?] |
| May I ...? | …してもいいですか？<br>[... shi te mo ī desu ka ?] |
| ..., please (polite request) | お願いします。<br>[onegai shi masu] |

| I'm looking for ... | …を探しています<br>[... wo sagashi te i masu] |
| restroom | トイレ<br>[toire] |
| ATM | ＡＴＭ<br>[ētīemu] |
| pharmacy (drugstore) | 薬局<br>[yakkyoku] |
| hospital | 病院<br>[byōin] |
| police station | 警察<br>[keisatsu] |
| subway | 地下鉄<br>[chikatetsu] |

| | |
|---|---|
| taxi | タクシー<br>[takushī] |
| train station | 駅<br>[eki] |

| | |
|---|---|
| My name is … | 私は…と申します<br>[watashi wa … to mōshi masu] |
| What's your name? | お名前は何ですか？<br>[o namae wa nan desu ka ?] |
| Could you please help me? | 助けていただけますか？<br>[tasuke te itadake masu ka ?] |
| I've got a problem. | 困ったことがあります。<br>[komatta koto ga arimasu] |
| I don't feel well. | 気分が悪いのです。<br>[kibun ga warui nodesu] |
| Call an ambulance! | 救急車を呼んで下さい！<br>[kyūkyū sha wo yon de kudasai !] |
| May I make a call? | 電話をしてもいいですか？<br>[denwa wo shi te mo ī desu ka ?] |

| | |
|---|---|
| I'm sorry. | ごめんなさい。<br>[gomennasai] |
| You're welcome. | どういたしまして。<br>[dōitashimashite] |

| | |
|---|---|
| I, me | 私<br>[watashi] |
| you (inform.) | 君<br>[kimi] |
| he | 彼<br>[kare] |
| she | 彼女<br>[kanojo] |
| they (masc.) | 彼ら<br>[karera] |
| they (fem.) | 彼女たち<br>[kanojotachi] |
| we | 私たち<br>[watashi tachi] |
| you (pl) | 君たち<br>[kimi tachi] |
| you (sg, form.) | あなた<br>[anata] |

| | |
|---|---|
| ENTRANCE | 入り口<br>[iriguchi] |
| EXIT | 出口<br>[deguchi] |
| OUT OF ORDER | 故障中<br>[koshō chū] |
| CLOSED | 休業中<br>[kyūgyō chū] |

| OPEN | 営業中 |
| | [eigyō chū] |
| FOR WOMEN | 女性用 |
| | [josei yō] |
| FOR MEN | 男性用 |
| | [dansei yō] |

## Questions

Where?
どこ？
[doko ?]

Where to?
どこへ？
[doko e ?]

Where from?
どこから？
[doko kara ?]

Why?
どうしてですか？
[dōshite desu ka ?]

For what reason?
なんのためですか？
[nan no tame desu ka ?]

When?
いつですか？
[i tsu desu ka ?]

How long?
どのぐらいですか？
[dono gurai desu ka ?]

At what time?
何時にですか？
[nan ji ni desu ka ?]

How much?
いくらですか？
[ikura desu ka ?]

Do you have ...?
…をお持ちですか？
[… wo o mochi desu ka ?]

Where is ...?
…はどこですか？
[… wa doko desu ka ?]

What time is it?
何時ですか？
[nan ji desu ka ?]

May I make a call?
電話をしてもいいですか？
[denwa wo shi te mo ī desu ka ?]

Who's there?
誰ですか？
[dare desu ka ?]

Can I smoke here?
ここでタバコを吸ってもいいですか？
[koko de tabako wo sutte mo ī desu ka ?]

May I ...?
…してもいいですか？
[… shi te mo ī desu ka ?]

## Needs

| | |
|---|---|
| I'd like … | …をしたいのですが<br>[… wo shi tai no desu ga] |
| I don't want … | …したくないです<br>[… shi taku nai desu] |
| I'm thirsty. | 喉が渇きました。<br>[nodo ga kawaki mashi ta] |
| I want to sleep. | 眠りたいです。<br>[nemuri tai desu] |

| | |
|---|---|
| I want … | したいです<br>[shi tai desu] |
| to wash up | 洗いたい<br>[arai tai] |
| to brush my teeth | 歯を磨きたい<br>[ha wo migaki tai] |
| to rest a while | しばらく休みたい<br>[shibaraku yasumi tai] |
| to change my clothes | 着替えたい<br>[kigae tai] |

| | |
|---|---|
| to go back to the hotel | ホテルに戻る<br>[hoteru ni modoru] |
| to buy … | …を買う<br>[… wo kau] |
| to go to … | …へ行く<br>[… e iku] |
| to visit … | …を訪問する<br>[… wo hōmon suru] |
| to meet with … | …と会う<br>[… to au] |
| to make a call | 電話をする<br>[denwa wo suru] |

| | |
|---|---|
| I'm tired. | 疲れています。<br>[tsukare te i masu] |
| We are tired. | 私たちは疲れました。<br>[watashi tachi wa tsukare mashita] |
| I'm cold. | 寒いです。<br>[samui desu] |
| I'm hot. | 暑いです。<br>[atsui desu] |
| I'm OK. | 大丈夫です。<br>[daijōbu desu] |

I need to make a call.          電話をしなければなりません。
                                [denwa wo shi nakere ba nari masen]

I need to go to the restroom.   トイレへ行きたいです。
                                [toire e iki tai desu]

I have to go.                   行かなければいけません。
                                [ika nakere ba ike masen]

I have to go now.               今すぐ行かなければいけません。
                                [ima sugu ika nakere ba ike masen]

## Asking for directions

| | |
|---|---|
| Excuse me, ... | すみません、… <br> [sumimasen, ...] |
| Where is ...? | …はどこですか？ <br> [... wa doko desu ka ?] |
| Which way is ...? | …はどちらですか？ <br> [...wa dochira desu ka ?] |
| Could you help me, please? | 助けていただけますか？ <br> [tasuke te itadake masu ka ?] |
| I'm looking for ... | …を探しています <br> [... wo sagashi te i masu] |
| I'm looking for the exit. | 出口を探しています。 <br> [deguchi wo sagashi te i masu] |
| I'm going to ... | …へ行く予定です <br> [... e iku yotei desu] |
| Am I going the right way to ...? | …へはこの道で合っていますか？ <br> [...e wa kono michi de atte i masu ka ?] |
| Is it far? | 遠いですか？ <br> [tōi desu ka ?] |
| Can I get there on foot? | そこまで歩いて行けますか？ <br> [soko made arui te ike masu ka ?] |
| Can you show me on the map? | 地図で教えて頂けますか？ <br> [chizu de oshie te itadake masu ka ?] |
| Show me where we are right now. | 今どこにいるかを教えて下さい。 <br> [ima doko ni iru ka wo oshie te kudasai] |
| Here | ここです <br> [koko desu] |
| There | あちらです <br> [achira desu] |
| This way | こちらです <br> [kochira desu] |
| Turn right. | 右に曲がって下さい。 <br> [migi ni magatte kudasai] |
| Turn left. | 左に曲がって下さい。 <br> [hidari ni magatte kudasai] |
| first (second, third) turn | 1つ目（2つ目、3つ目） <br> の曲がり角 <br> [hitotsume (futatsume, mittsume) <br> no magarikado] |
| to the right | 右に <br> [migi ni] |

to the left

左に
[hidari ni]

Go straight.

まっすぐ歩いて下さい。
[massugu arui te kudasai]

# Signs

| | |
|---|---|
| WELCOME! | いらっしゃいませ！<br>[irasshai mase !] |
| ENTRANCE | 入り口<br>[iriguchi] |
| EXIT | 出口<br>[deguchi] |
| PUSH | 押す<br>[osu] |
| PULL | 引く<br>[hiku] |
| OPEN | 営業中<br>[eigyō chū] |
| CLOSED | 休業中<br>[kyūgyō chū] |
| FOR WOMEN | 女性用<br>[josei yō] |
| FOR MEN | 男性用<br>[dansei yō] |
| MEN, GENTS | 男性用<br>[dansei yō] |
| WOMEN, LADIES | 女性用<br>[josei yō] |
| DISCOUNTS | 営業<br>[eigyō] |
| SALE | セール<br>[sēru] |
| FREE | 無料<br>[muryō] |
| NEW! | 新商品！<br>[shin shōhin !] |
| ATTENTION! | 目玉品！<br>[medama hin !] |
| NO VACANCIES | 満員<br>[man in] |
| RESERVED | ご予約済み<br>[go yoyaku zumi] |
| ADMINISTRATION | 管理<br>[kanri] |
| STAFF ONLY | 社員専用<br>[shain senyō] |

BEWARE OF THE DOG!
猛犬注意
[mōken chūi]

NO SMOKING!
禁煙！
[kin en !]

DO NOT TOUCH!
触るな危険！
[sawaru na kiken !]

DANGEROUS
危ない
[abunai]

DANGER
危険
[kiken]

HIGH VOLTAGE
高電圧
[kō denatsu]

NO SWIMMING!
水泳禁止！
[suiei kinshi !]

OUT OF ORDER
故障中
[koshō chū]

FLAMMABLE
火気注意
[kaki chūi]

FORBIDDEN
禁止
[kinshi]

NO TRESPASSING!
通り抜け禁止！
[tōrinuke kinshi !]

WET PAINT
ペンキ塗り立て
[penki nuritate]

CLOSED FOR RENOVATIONS
改装閉鎖中
[kaisō heisa chū]

WORKS AHEAD
この先工事中
[kono saki kōji chū]

DETOUR
迂回
[ukai]

## Transportation. General phrases

| | |
|---|---|
| plane | 飛行機<br>[hikōki] |
| train | 電車<br>[densha] |
| bus | バス<br>[basu] |
| ferry | フェリー<br>[ferī] |
| taxi | タクシー<br>[takushī] |
| car | 車<br>[kuruma] |

| | |
|---|---|
| schedule | 時刻表<br>[jikoku hyō] |
| Where can I see the schedule? | どこで時刻表を見られますか？<br>[doko de jikoku hyō wo mirare masu ka ?] |
| workdays (weekdays) | 平日<br>[heijitsu] |
| weekends | 週末<br>[shūmatsu] |
| holidays | 祝日<br>[kokumin no syukujitsu] |

| | |
|---|---|
| DEPARTURE | 出発<br>[shuppatsu] |
| ARRIVAL | 到着<br>[tōchaku] |
| DELAYED | 遅延<br>[chien] |
| CANCELED | 欠航<br>[kekkō] |

| | |
|---|---|
| next (train, etc.) | 次の<br>[tsugi no] |
| first | 最初の<br>[saisho no] |
| last | 最後の<br>[saigono] |

| | |
|---|---|
| When is the next ...? | 次の…はいつですか？<br>[tsugi no ... wa i tsu desu ka ?] |
| When is the first ...? | 最初の…はいつですか？<br>[saisho no ... wa i tsu desu ka ?] |

When is the last ...?　　　　　　　　最後の…はいつですか？
　　　　　　　　　　　　　　　　　[saigo no ... wa i tsu desu ka ?]

transfer (change of trains, etc.)　　乗り継ぎ
　　　　　　　　　　　　　　　　　[noritsugi]

to make a transfer　　　　　　　　乗り継ぎをする
　　　　　　　　　　　　　　　　　[noritsugi wo suru]

Do I need to make a transfer?　　　乗り継ぎをする必要がありますか？
　　　　　　　　　　　　　　　　　[noritsugi o suru hitsuyō ga ari masu ka ?]

## Buying tickets

| | |
|---|---|
| Where can I buy tickets? | どこで乗車券を買えますか？<br>[doko de jōsha ken wo kae masu ka ?] |
| ticket | 乗車券<br>[jōsha ken] |
| to buy a ticket | 乗車券を買う<br>[jōsha ken wo kau] |
| ticket price | 乗車券の値段<br>[jōsha ken no nedan] |
| Where to? | どこへ？<br>[doko e ?] |
| To what station? | どこの駅へ？<br>[doko no eki e ?] |
| I need ... | …が必要です<br>[... ga hitsuyō desu] |
| one ticket | 券　1枚<br>[ken ichi mai] |
| two tickets | 2枚<br>[ni mai] |
| three tickets | 3枚<br>[san mai] |
| one-way | 片道<br>[katamichi] |
| round-trip | 往復<br>[ōfuku] |
| first class | ファーストクラス<br>[fāsuto kurasu] |
| second class | エコノミークラス<br>[ekonomī kurasu] |
| today | 今日<br>[kyō] |
| tomorrow | 明日<br>[ashita] |
| the day after tomorrow | あさって<br>[asatte] |
| in the morning | 朝に<br>[asa ni] |
| in the afternoon | 昼に<br>[hiru ni] |
| in the evening | 晩に<br>[ban ni] |

aisle seat

通路側の席
[tsūro gawa no seki]

window seat

窓側の席
[madogawa no seki]

How much?

いくらですか？
[ikura desu ka ?]

Can I pay by credit card?

カードで支払いができますか？
[kādo de shiharai ga deki masu ka ?]

# Bus

| | |
|---|---|
| bus | バス<br>[basu] |
| intercity bus | 高速バス<br>[kōsoku basu] |
| bus stop | バス停<br>[basutei] |
| Where's the nearest bus stop? | 最寄りのバス停はどこですか？<br>[moyori no basutei wa doko desu ka ?] |
| number (bus ~, etc.) | 数<br>[kazu] |
| Which bus do I take to get to ...? | …に行くにはどのバスに乗れば<br>いいですか ？<br>[…ni iku niwa dono basu ni nore ba<br>ī desu ka …?] |
| Does this bus go to ...? | このバスは…まで行きますか？<br>[kono basu wa … made iki masu ka ?] |
| How frequent are the buses? | バスはどのくらいの頻度で<br>来ますか？<br>[basu wa dono kurai no hindo de<br>ki masu ka?] |
| every 15 minutes | １５分おき<br>[jyū go fun oki] |
| every half hour | ３０分おき<br>[sanjuppun oki] |
| every hour | １時間に １回<br>[ichi jikan ni ittu kai] |
| several times a day | １日に数回<br>[ichi nichi ni sū kai] |
| ... times a day | １日に…回<br>[ichi nichi ni … kai] |
| schedule | 時刻表<br>[jikoku hyō] |
| Where can I see the schedule? | どこで時刻表を見られますか？<br>[doko de jikoku hyō wo mirare masu ka ?] |
| When is the next bus? | 次のバスは何時ですか？<br>[tsugi no basu wa nan ji desu ka ?] |
| When is the first bus? | 最初のバスは何時ですか？<br>[saisho no basu wa nan ji desu ka ?] |
| When is the last bus? | 最後のバスは何時ですか？<br>[saigo no basu wa nan ji desu ka ?] |

stop

バス停、停留所
[basutei, teiryūjo]

next stop

次のバス停、次の停留所
[tsugi no basutei, tsugi no teiryūjo]

last stop (terminus)

最終停留所
[saishū teiryūjo]

Stop here, please.

ここで止めてください。
[koko de tome te kudasai]

Excuse me, this is my stop.

すみません、ここで降ります。
[sumimasen, koko de ori masu]

# Train

| | |
|---|---|
| train | 電車<br>[densha] |
| suburban train | 郊外電車<br>[kōgai densha] |
| long-distance train | 長距離列車<br>[chōkyori ressha] |
| train station | 電車の駅<br>[densha no eki] |
| Excuse me, where is the exit to the platform? | すみません、ホームへはど<br>う行けばいいですか？<br>[sumimasen, hōmu e wa dō<br>ike ba ī desu ka?] |
| Does this train go to ...? | この電車は…まで行きますか？<br>[kono densha wa ... made iki masu ka ?] |
| next train | 次の駅<br>[tsugi no eki] |
| When is the next train? | 次の電車は何時ですか？<br>[tsugi no densha wa nan ji desu ka ?] |
| Where can I see the schedule? | どこで時刻表を見られますか？<br>[doko de jikoku hyō wo mirare masu ka ?] |
| From which platform? | どのホームからですか？<br>[dono hōmu kara desu ka ?] |
| When does the train arrive in ...? | 電車はいつ到着しますか…？<br>[densha wa i tsu tōchaku<br>shi masu ka ...?] |
| Please help me. | 助けて下さい。<br>[tasuke te kudasai] |
| I'm looking for my seat. | 私の座席を探しています。<br>[watashi no zaseki wo sagashi te i masu] |
| We're looking for our seats. | 私たちの座席を探し<br>ています。<br>[watashi tachi no zaseki wo sagashi<br>te i masu] |
| My seat is taken. | 私の席に他の人が<br>座っています。<br>[watashi no seki ni hoka no hito ga<br>suwatte i masu] |
| Our seats are taken. | 私たちの席に他の人が<br>座っています。<br>[watashi tachi no seki ni hoka no hito ga<br>suwatte i masu.] |

I'm sorry but this is my seat.　　　すみませんが、こちらは私
　　　　　　　　　　　　　　　　の席です。
　　　　　　　　　　　　　　　　[sumimasen ga, kochira wa watashi
　　　　　　　　　　　　　　　　no seki desu]

Is this seat taken?　　　　　　　この席はふさがっていますか？
　　　　　　　　　　　　　　　　[kono seki wa husagatte i masu ka ?]

May I sit here?　　　　　　　　　ここに座ってもいいですか？
　　　　　　　　　　　　　　　　[koko ni suwatte mo ī desu ka ?]

## On the train. Dialogue (No ticket)

Ticket, please.
乗車券を見せて下さい。
[jōsha ken wo mise te kudasai]

I don't have a ticket.
乗車券を持っていません。
[jōsha ken wo motte i masen]

I lost my ticket.
乗車券を失くしました。
[jōsha ken wo nakushi mashi ta]

I forgot my ticket at home.
乗車券を家に忘れました。
[jōsha ken wo ie ni wasure mashi ta]

You can buy a ticket from me.
私からも乗車券を購入できます。
[watashi kara mo jōsha ken wo kōnyū deki masu]

You will also have to pay a fine.
それから罰金を払わなけれ
ばいけません。
[sorekara bakkin wo harawa nakere ba ike masen]

Okay.
わかりました。
[wakari mashi ta]

Where are you going?
行き先はどこですか？
[yukisaki wa doko desu ka ?]

I'm going to …
…に行きます。
[… ni iki masu]

How much? I don't understand.
いくらですか？ わかりません。
[ikura desu ka ? wakari masen]

Write it down, please.
書いてください。
[kai te kudasai]

Okay. Can I pay with a credit card?
わかりました。クレジットカード
で支払いできますか？
[wakari mashi ta. kurejittokādo de shiharaideki masu ka?]

Yes, you can.
はい。
[hai]

Here's your receipt.
レシートです。
[reshīto desu]

Sorry about the fine.
罰金をいただいてすみません。
[bakkin wo itadaite sumimasen]

That's okay. It was my fault.
大丈夫です。私のせいですから。
[daijōbu desu. watashi no sei desu kara]

Enjoy your trip.
良い旅を。
[yoi tabi wo]

## Taxi

| | |
|---|---|
| taxi | タクシー<br>[takushī] |
| taxi driver | タクシー運転手<br>[takushī unten shu] |
| to catch a taxi | タクシーをひろう<br>[takushī wo hirō] |
| taxi stand | タクシー乗り場<br>[takushī noriba] |
| Where can I get a taxi? | どこでタクシーをひろえますか？<br>[doko de takushī wo hiroe masu ka ?] |
| to call a taxi | タクシーを呼ぶ<br>[takushī wo yobu] |
| I need a taxi. | タクシーが必要です。<br>[takushī ga hitsuyō desu] |
| Right now. | 今すぐ。<br>[ima sugu] |
| What is your address (location)? | 住所はどこですか？<br>[jūsho wa doko desu ka ?] |
| My address is … | 私の住所は…です<br>[watashi no jūsho wa … desu] |
| Your destination? | どちらへ行かれますか？<br>[dochira e ikare masu ka ?] |
| Excuse me, … | すみません、…<br>[sumimasen, …] |
| Are you available? | 乗ってもいいですか？<br>[nottemo ī desu ka ?] |
| How much is it to get to …? | …までいくらですか？<br>[… made ikura desu ka ?] |
| Do you know where it is? | どこにあるかご存知ですか？<br>[doko ni aru ka gozonji desu ka ?] |
| Airport, please. | 空港へお願いします。<br>[kūkō e onegai shi masu] |
| Stop here, please. | ここで止めてください。<br>[koko de tome te kudasai] |
| It's not here. | ここではありません。<br>[koko de wa ari masen] |
| This is the wrong address. | その住所は間違っています。<br>[sono jūsho wa machigatte i masu] |
| Turn left. | 左へ曲がって下さい<br>[hidari e magatte kudasai] |
| Turn right. | 右へ曲がって下さい<br>[migi e magatte kudasai] |

| How much do I owe you? | いくらですか？ |
| | [ikura desu ka ?] |
| I'd like a receipt, please. | 領収書を下さい。 |
| | [ryōshū sho wo kudasai] |
| Keep the change. | おつりはいりません。 |
| | [o tsuri hairi masen] |

| Would you please wait for me? | 待っていて頂けますか？ |
| | [matte i te itadake masu ka?] |
| five minutes | 5分 |
| | [go fun] |
| ten minutes | 10分 |
| | [juppun] |
| fifteen minutes | 15分 |
| | [jyū go fun] |
| twenty minutes | 20分 |
| | [nijuppun] |
| half an hour | 30分 |
| | [sanjuppun] |

# Hotel

| | |
|---|---|
| Hello. | こんにちは。<br>[konnichiwa] |
| My name is ... | 私の名前は…です<br>[watashi no namae wa ... desu] |
| I have a reservation. | 予約をしました。<br>[yoyaku wo shi mashi ta] |
| I need ... | 私は…が必要です<br>[watashi wa ... ga hitsuyō desu] |
| a single room | シングルルーム<br>[shinguru rūmu] |
| a double room | ツインルーム<br>[tsuin rūmu] |
| How much is that? | いくらですか?<br>[ikura desu ka ?] |
| That's a bit expensive. | それは少し高いです。<br>[sore wa sukoshi takai desu] |
| Do you have any other options? | 他にも選択肢はありますか?<br>[hoka ni mo sentakushi wa ari masu ka ?] |
| I'll take it. | それにします。<br>[sore ni shi masu] |
| I'll pay in cash. | 現金で払います。<br>[genkin de harai masu] |
| I've got a problem. | 困ったことがあります。<br>[komatta koto ga arimasu] |
| My ... is broken. | 私の…が壊れています。<br>[watashi no ... ga koware te i masu] |
| My ... is out of order. | 私の…が故障しています。<br>[watashi no ... ga koshō shi te i masu] |
| TV | テレビ<br>[terebi] |
| air conditioning | エアコン<br>[eakon] |
| tap | 蛇口<br>[jaguchi] |
| shower | シャワー<br>[shawā] |
| sink | 流し台<br>[nagashi dai] |
| safe | 金庫<br>[kinko] |

| | |
|---|---|
| door lock | 錠<br>[jō] |
| electrical outlet | 電気のコンセント<br>[dengen no konsento] |
| hairdryer | ドライヤー<br>[doraiyā] |

| | |
|---|---|
| I don't have ... | …がありません<br>[… ga ari masen] |
| water | 水<br>[mizu] |
| light | 明かり<br>[akari] |
| electricity | 電気<br>[denki] |

| | |
|---|---|
| Can you give me ...? | …を頂けませんか？<br>[… wo itadake masenka ?] |
| a towel | タオル<br>[taoru] |
| a blanket | 毛布<br>[mōfu] |
| slippers | スリッパ<br>[surippa] |
| a robe | バスローブ<br>[basurōbu] |
| shampoo | シャンプーを何本か<br>[shanpū wo nannbon ka] |
| soap | 石鹸をいくつか<br>[sekken wo ikutsu ka] |

| | |
|---|---|
| I'd like to change rooms. | 部屋を変えたいのですが。<br>[heya wo kae tai no desu ga] |
| I can't find my key. | 鍵が見つかりません。<br>[kagi ga mitsukarimasenn] |
| Could you open my room, please? | 部屋を開けて頂けますか？<br>[heya wo ake te itadake masu ka ?] |
| Who's there? | 誰ですか？<br>[dare desu ka ?] |
| Come in! | どうぞお入り下さい<br>[dōzo o hairikudasai] |
| Just a minute! | 少々お待ち下さい！<br>[shōshō omachi kudasai !] |
| Not right now, please. | 後にしてもらえますか。<br>[ato ni shi te morae masu ka] |

| | |
|---|---|
| Come to my room, please. | 私の部屋に来て下さい。<br>[watashi no heya ni ki te kudasai] |
| I'd like to order food service. | 食事サービスをお願いしたい<br>のですが。<br>[shokuji sābisu wo onegai shi tai<br>no desu ga] |

My room number is …　私の部屋の番号は…
[watashi no heya no bangō wa …]

I'm leaving …　チェックアウトします…
[tyekkuauto shi masu …]

We're leaving …　私たちはチェックアウトします…
[watashi tachi wa tyekkuauto shi masu …]

right now　今すぐ
[ima sugu]

this afternoon　今日の午後
[kyō no gogo]

tonight　今晩
[konban]

tomorrow　明日
[ashita]

tomorrow morning　明日の朝
[ashita no asa]

tomorrow evening　明日の夕方
[ashita no yūgata]

the day after tomorrow　あさって
[asatte]

I'd like to pay.　支払いをしたいのですが。
[shiharai wo shi tai no desu ga]

Everything was wonderful.　何もかもがよかったです。
[nanimokamo ga yokatta desu]

Where can I get a taxi?　どこでタクシーをひろえますか？
[doko de takushī wo hiroe masu ka ?]

Would you call a taxi for me, please?　タクシーを呼んでいただけますか？
[takushī wo yon de itadake masu ka ?]

## Restaurant

| | |
|---|---|
| Can I look at the menu, please? | メニューを頂けますか？<br>[menyū wo itadake masu ka ?] |
| Table for one. | 一人用の席をお願いします。<br>[hitori yō no seki wo onegai shimasu] |
| There are two (three, four) of us. | 2人（3人、4人）です。<br>[futari (san nin, yon nin) desu] |

| | |
|---|---|
| Smoking | 喫煙<br>[kitsuen] |
| No smoking | 禁煙<br>[kinen] |
| Excuse me! (addressing a waiter) | すみません！<br>[sumimasen !] |
| menu | メニュー<br>[menyū] |
| wine list | ワインリスト<br>[wain risuto] |
| The menu, please. | メニューを下さい。<br>[menyū wo kudasai] |

| | |
|---|---|
| Are you ready to order? | ご注文をお伺いしても<br>よろしいですか？<br>[go chūmon wo o ukagai shi te mo<br>yoroshī desu ka?] |
| What will you have? | ご注文は何にしますか？<br>[go chūmon wa nani ni shi masu ka ?] |
| I'll have … | …を下さい。<br>[… wo kudasai] |

| | |
|---|---|
| I'm a vegetarian. | 私はベジタリアンです。<br>[watashi wa bejitarian desu] |
| meat | 肉<br>[niku] |
| fish | 魚<br>[sakana] |
| vegetables | 野菜<br>[yasai] |
| Do you have vegetarian dishes? | ベジタリアン向けの料理はありますか？<br>[bejitarian muke no ryōri<br>wa ari masu ka?] |
| I don't eat pork. | 私は豚肉を食べません。<br>[watashi wa butaniku o tabe masen] |

He /she/ doesn't eat meat.
彼 /彼女/ は肉を食べません。
[kare /kanojo/ wa niku o tabe masen]

I am allergic to ...
私は…にアレルギーがあります
[watashi wa ... ni arerugī ga ari masu]

Would you please bring me ...
…を持ってきてもらえますか
[... wo motte ki te morae masu ka]

salt | pepper | sugar
塩 | 胡椒 | 砂糖
[shio | koshō | satō]

coffee | tea | dessert
コーヒー | お茶 | デザート
[kōhī | ocha | dezāto]

water | sparkling | plain
水 | スパークリングウォーター | 真水
[mizu | supāku ringu wōtā | mamizu]

a spoon | fork | knife
スプーン | フォーク | ナイフ
[supūn | fōku | naifu]

a plate | napkin
プレート | ナプキン
[purēto | napukin]

Enjoy your meal!
どうぞお召し上がりください
[dōzo omeshiagari kudasai]

One more, please.
もう一つお願いします。
[mō hitotsu onegai shi masu]

It was very delicious.
とても美味しかったです。
[totemo oishikatta desu]

check | change | tip
勘定 | おつり | チップ
[kanjō | o tsuri | chippu]

Check, please.
(Could I have the check, please?)
お勘定をお願いします。
[o kanjō wo onegai shi masu]

Can I pay by credit card?
カードで支払いができますか？
[kādo de shiharai ga deki masu ka ?]

I'm sorry, there's a mistake here.
すみません、間違いがあります。
[sumimasen, machigai ga ari masu]

# Shopping

| | |
|---|---|
| Can I help you? | いらっしゃいませ。<br>[irasshai mase] |
| Do you have ...? | …をお持ちですか？<br>[... wo o mochi desu ka ?] |
| I'm looking for ... | …を探しています<br>[... wo sagashi te i masu] |
| I need ... | …が必要です<br>[... ga hitsuyō desu] |
| I'm just looking. | ただ見ているだけです。<br>[tada mi te iru dake desu] |
| We're just looking. | 私たちはただ見ているだけです。<br>[watashi tachi wa tada mi te iru<br>dake desu] |
| I'll come back later. | また後で来ます。<br>[mata atode ki masu] |
| We'll come back later. | また後で来ます。<br>[mata atode ki masu] |
| discounts \| sale | 値引き ｜ セール<br>[nebiki \| sēru] |
| Would you please show me ... | …を見せていただけますか<br>[... wo mise te itadake masu ka] |
| Would you please give me ... | …をいただけますか<br>[... wo itadake masu ka] |
| Can I try it on? | 試着できますか？<br>[shichaku deki masu ka ?] |
| Excuse me, where's the fitting room? | すみません、試着室は<br>どこですか？<br>[sumimasen, shichaku shitsu wa<br>doko desu ka?] |
| Which color would you like? | どの色がお好みですか？<br>[dono iro ga o konomi desu ka ?] |
| size \| length | サイズ ｜ 長さ<br>[saizu \| naga sa] |
| How does it fit? | サイズは合いましたか？<br>[saizu wa ai mashi ta ka ?] |
| How much is it? | これはいくらですか？<br>[kore wa ikura desu ka ?] |
| That's too expensive. | 高すぎます。<br>[takasugi masu] |

I'll take it.

これにします。
[kore ni shi masu]

Excuse me, where do I pay?

すみません、どこで支払いますか？
[sumimasen, doko de shiharai masu ka ?]

Will you pay in cash or credit card?

現金とクレジットカードのどちら
でお支払いされますか？
[genkin to kurejittokādo no dochira
de o shiharai sare masu ka?]

In cash | with credit card

現金 | クレジットカード
[genkin | kurejittokādo]

Do you want the receipt?

レシートはお入り用ですか？
[reshīto ha oiriyō desu ka ?]

Yes, please.

お願いします。
[onegai shi masu]

No, it's OK.

いえ、結構です。
[ie, kekkō desu]

Thank you. Have a nice day!

ありがとうございます。良い一日を！
[arigatō gozai masu. yoi ichi nichi wo !]

# In town

| | |
|---|---|
| Excuse me, please. | すみません、… <br> [sumimasen, ...] |
| I'm looking for ... | …を探しています <br> [watashi wa ... wo sagashi te i masu] |
| the subway | 地下鉄 <br> [chikatetsu] |
| my hotel | ホテル <br> [hoteru] |
| the movie theater | 映画館 <br> [eiga kan] |
| a taxi stand | タクシー乗り場 <br> [takushī noriba] |
| an ATM | ATM <br> [ētīemu] |
| a foreign exchange office | 両替所 <br> [ryōgae sho] |
| an internet café | インターネットカフェ <br> [intānetto kafe] |
| ... street | …通り <br> [... tōri] |
| this place | この場所 <br> [kono basho] |
| Do you know where ... is? | …がどこにあるかご存知ですか？ <br> [... ga doko ni aru ka gozonji desu ka ?] |
| Which street is this? | この通りの名前は何ですか？ <br> [kono michi no namae wa nani desu ka ?] |
| Show me where we are right now. | 今どこにいるかを教えて下さい。 <br> [ima doko ni iru ka wo oshie te kudasai] |
| Can I get there on foot? | そこまで歩いて行けますか？ <br> [soko made arui te ike masu ka?] |
| Do you have a map of the city? | 市内地図をお持ちですか？ <br> [shinai chizu wo o mochi desu ka ?] |
| How much is a ticket to get in? | チケットはいくらですか？ <br> [chiketto wa ikura desu ka ?] |
| Can I take pictures here? | ここで写真を撮ってもいいですか？ <br> [koko de shashin wo totte mo ī desu ka ?] |
| Are you open? | 開いていますか？ <br> [hirai te i masu ka ?] |

When do you open?

何時に開きますか？
[nan ji ni hiraki masu ka ?]

When do you close?

何時に閉まりますか？
[nan ji ni shimari masu ka ?]

# Money

| | |
|---|---|
| money | お金<br>[okane] |
| cash | 現金<br>[genkin] |
| paper money | 紙幣<br>[shihei] |
| loose change | おつり<br>[o tsuri] |
| check \| change \| tip | 勘定 ｜ おつり ｜ チップ<br>[kanjō \| o tsuri \| chippu] |

| | |
|---|---|
| credit card | クレジットカード<br>[kurejittokādo] |
| wallet | 財布<br>[saifu] |
| to buy | 買う<br>[kau] |
| to pay | 支払う<br>[shiharau] |
| fine | 罰金<br>[bakkin] |
| free | 無料<br>[muryō] |

| | |
|---|---|
| Where can I buy ...? | …はどこで買えますか？<br>[… wa doko de kae masu ka ?] |
| Is the bank open now? | 銀行は今開いていますか？<br>[ginkō wa ima hirai te i masu ka ?] |
| When does it open? | いつ開きますか？<br>[itsu hiraki masu ka ?] |
| When does it close? | いつ閉まりますか？<br>[itsu shimari masu ka ?] |

| | |
|---|---|
| How much? | いくらですか？<br>[ikura desu ka ?] |
| How much is this? | これはいくらですか？<br>[kore wa ikura desu ka ?] |
| That's too expensive. | 高すぎます。<br>[takasugi masu] |

| | |
|---|---|
| Excuse me, where do I pay? | すみません、レジはどこですか？<br>[sumimasen, reji wa doko desu ka ?] |
| Check, please. | 勘定をお願いします。<br>[kanjō wo onegai shi masu] |

Can I pay by credit card?　　　　　　　カードで支払いができますか？
　　　　　　　　　　　　　　　　　　　[kādo de shiharai ga deki masu ka ?]

Is there an ATM here?　　　　　　　　　ここにＡＴＭはありますか？
　　　　　　　　　　　　　　　　　　　[kokoni ētīemu wa ari masu ka ?]

I'm looking for an ATM.　　　　　　　　ＡＴＭを探しています。
　　　　　　　　　　　　　　　　　　　[ētīemu wo sagashi te i masu]

I'm looking for a foreign exchange office.　両替所を探しています。
　　　　　　　　　　　　　　　　　　　[ryōgae sho wo sagashi te i masu]

I'd like to change …　　　　　　　　　　両替をしたいのですが…
　　　　　　　　　　　　　　　　　　　[ryōgae wo shi tai no desu ga…]

What is the exchange rate?　　　　　　為替レートはいくらですか？
　　　　　　　　　　　　　　　　　　　[kawase rēto wa ikura desu ka ?]

Do you need my passport?　　　　　　　パスポートは必要ですか？
　　　　　　　　　　　　　　　　　　　[pasupōto ha hituyō desu ka ?]

# Time

| | |
|---|---|
| What time is it? | 何時ですか？<br>[nan ji desu ka ?] |
| When? | いつですか？<br>[i tsu desu ka ?] |
| At what time? | 何時にですか？<br>[nan ji ni desu ka ?] |
| now \| later \| after … | 今 ｜ 1後で ｜ …の後<br>[ima \|ato de \| … no ato] |
| one o'clock | 1時<br>[ichi ji] |
| one fifteen | 1時 15分<br>[ichi ji jyū go fun] |
| one thirty | 1時半<br>[ichi ji han] |
| one forty-five | 1時45分<br>[ichi ji yon jyū go fun] |
| one \| two \| three | 1 ｜ 2 ｜ 3<br>[ichi \| ni \| san] |
| four \| five \| six | 4 ｜ 5 ｜ 6<br>[yonn \| go \|roku] |
| seven \| eight \| nine | 7 ｜ 8 ｜ 9<br>[shichi \| hachi \| kyū] |
| ten \| eleven \| twelve | 10 ｜ 11 ｜ 12<br>[jyū \| jyūichi \| jyūni] |
| in … | …後<br>[… go] |
| five minutes | 5分<br>[go fun] |
| ten minutes | 10分<br>[juppun] |
| fifteen minutes | 15分<br>[jyū go fun] |
| twenty minutes | 20分<br>[nijuppun] |
| half an hour | 30分<br>[sanjuppun] |
| an hour | 一時間<br>[ichi jikan] |

| | |
|---|---|
| in the morning | 朝に<br>[asa ni] |
| early in the morning | 早朝<br>[sōchō] |
| this morning | 今朝<br>[kesa] |
| tomorrow morning | 明日の朝<br>[ashita no asa] |
| at noon | ランチのときに<br>[ranchi no toki ni] |
| in the afternoon | 午後に<br>[gogo ni] |
| in the evening | 夕方<br>[yūgata] |
| tonight | 今夜<br>[konya] |
| at night | 夜<br>[yoru] |
| yesterday | 昨日<br>[kinō] |
| today | 今日<br>[kyō] |
| tomorrow | 明日<br>[ashita] |
| the day after tomorrow | あさって<br>[asatte] |
| What day is it today? | 今日は何曜日ですか？<br>[kyō wa nan yōbi desu ka ?] |
| It's ... | …です<br>[… desu] |
| Monday | 月曜日<br>[getsuyōbi] |
| Tuesday | 火曜日<br>[kayōbi] |
| Wednesday | 水曜日<br>[suiyōbi] |
| Thursday | 木曜日<br>[mokuyōbi] |
| Friday | 金曜日<br>[kinyōbi] |
| Saturday | 土曜日<br>[doyōbi] |
| Sunday | 日曜日<br>[nichiyōbi] |

## Greetings. Introductions

| | |
|---|---|
| Hello. | こんにちは。<br>[konnichiwa] |
| Pleased to meet you. | お会いできて嬉しいです。<br>[o aideki te ureshī desu] |
| Me too. | こちらこそ。<br>[kochira koso] |
| I'd like you to meet … | …さんに会わせていただきたいのですが<br>[… san ni awasete itadaki tai no desu ga] |
| Nice to meet you. | 初めまして。<br>[hajime mashite] |

| | |
|---|---|
| How are you? | お元気ですか？<br>[o genki desu ka ?] |
| My name is … | 私の名前は…です<br>[watashi no namae wa … desu] |
| His name is … | 彼の名前は…です<br>[kare no namae wa … desu] |
| Her name is … | 彼女の名前は…です<br>[kanojo no namae wa … desu] |
| What's your name? | お名前は何ですか？<br>[o namae wa nan desu ka ?] |
| What's his name? | 彼の名前は何ですか？<br>[kare no namae wa nan desu ka ?] |
| What's her name? | 彼女の名前は何ですか？<br>[kanojo no namae wa nan desu ka ?] |

| | |
|---|---|
| What's your last name? | 苗字は何ですか？<br>[myōji wa nan desu ka ?] |
| You can call me … | …と呼んで下さい<br>[… to yon de kudasai] |
| Where are you from? | ご出身はどちらですか？<br>[go shusshin wa dochira desu ka ?] |
| I'm from … | …の出身です<br>[… no shusshin desu] |
| What do you do for a living? | お仕事は何をされていますか？<br>[o shigoto wa nani wo sare te i masu ka ?] |
| Who is this? | 誰ですか？<br>[dare desu ka ?] |
| Who is he? | 彼は誰ですか？<br>[kare wa dare desu ka ?] |
| Who is she? | 彼女は誰ですか？<br>[kanojo wa dare desu ka ?] |
| Who are they? | 彼らは誰ですか？<br>[karera wa dare desu ka ?] |

This is ...
こちらは…
[kochira wa …]

my friend (masc.)
私の友達です
[watashi no tomodachi desu]

my friend (fem.)
私の友達です
[watashi no tomodachi desu]

my husband
私の主人です
[watashi no shujin desu]

my wife
私の妻です
[watashi no tsuma desu]

my father
私の父です
[watashi no chichi desu]

my mother
私の母です
[watashi no haha desu]

my brother
私の兄です
[watashi no ani desu]

my sister
私の妹です
[watashi no imōto desu]

my son
私の息子です
[watashi no musuko desu]

my daughter
私の娘です
[watashi no musume desu]

This is our son.
私たちの息子です。
[watashi tachi no musuko desu]

This is our daughter.
私たちの娘です。
[watashi tachi no musume desu]

These are my children.
私の子供です。
[watashi no kodomo desu]

These are our children.
私たちの子供です。
[watashi tachi no kodomo desu]

# Farewells

| | |
|---|---|
| Good bye! | さようなら！<br>[sayōnara !] |
| Bye! (inform.) | じゃあね！<br>[jā ne !] |
| See you tomorrow. | また明日。<br>[mata ashita] |
| See you soon. | またね。<br>[mata ne] |
| See you at seven. | 7時に会おう。<br>[shichi ji ni ao u] |
| Have fun! | 楽しんでね！<br>[tanoshin de ne !] |
| Talk to you later. | じゃあ後で。<br>[jā atode] |
| Have a nice weekend. | 良い週末を。<br>[yoi shūmatsu wo] |
| Good night. | お休みなさい。<br>[o yasuminasai] |
| It's time for me to go. | もう時間です。<br>[mō jikan desu] |
| I have to go. | もう行かなければなりません。<br>[mō ika nakere ba nari masen] |
| I will be right back. | すぐ戻ります。<br>[sugu modori masu] |
| It's late. | もう遅いです。<br>[mō osoi desu] |
| I have to get up early. | 早く起きなければいけません。<br>[hayaku oki nakere ba ike masen] |
| I'm leaving tomorrow. | 明日出発します。<br>[ashita shuppatsu shi masu] |
| We're leaving tomorrow. | 私たちは明日出発します。<br>[watashi tachi wa ashita shuppatsu shi masu] |
| Have a nice trip! | 旅行を楽しんで下さい！<br>[ryokō wo tanoshin de kudasai !] |
| It was nice meeting you. | お会いできて嬉しかったです。<br>[o shiriai ni nare te uresikatta desu] |
| It was nice talking to you. | お話できて良かったです。<br>[ohanashi deki te yokatta desu] |

Thanks for everything.  色々とありがとうございました。
[iroiro to arigatō gozai mashi ta]

I had a very good time.  とても楽しかったです。
[totemo tanoshikatta desu]

We had a very good time.  とても楽しかったです。
[totemo tanoshikatta desu]

It was really great.  とても楽しかった。
[totemo tanoshikatta]

I'm going to miss you.  寂しくなります。
[sabishiku nari masu]

We're going to miss you.  寂しくなります。
[sabishiku nari masu]

Good luck!  幸運を祈るよ！
[kōun wo inoru yo !]

Say hi to …  …に宜しくお伝え下さい。
[… ni yoroshiku otsutae kudasai]

## Foreign language

| | |
|---|---|
| I don't understand. | 分かりません。<br>[wakari masen] |
| Write it down, please. | それを書いて頂けますか？<br>[sore wo kai te itadake masu ka ?] |
| Do you speak ...? | …語で話せますか？<br>[… go de hanase masu ka ?] |
| I speak a little bit of ... | …を少し話せます<br>[…wo sukoshi hanase masu] |
| English | 英語<br>[eigo] |
| Turkish | トルコ語<br>[toruko go] |
| Arabic | アラビア語<br>[arabia go] |
| French | フランス語<br>[furansu go] |
| German | ドイツ語<br>[doitsu go] |
| Italian | イタリア語<br>[itaria go] |
| Spanish | スペイン語<br>[supein go] |
| Portuguese | ポルトガル語<br>[porutogaru go] |
| Chinese | 中国語<br>[chūgoku go] |
| Japanese | 日本語<br>[nihon go] |
| Can you repeat that, please. | もう一度言っていただけますか。<br>[mōichido itte itadake masuka] |
| I understand. | 分かりました。<br>[wakari mashi ta] |
| I don't understand. | 分かりません。<br>[wakari masen] |
| Please speak more slowly. | もう少しゆっくり話して下さい。<br>[mōsukoshi yukkuri hanashi te kudasai] |
| Is that correct? (Am I saying it right?) | これで合っていますか？<br>[kore de atte i masu ka ?] |
| What is this? (What does this mean?) | これは何ですか？<br>[kore wa nan desu ka ?] |

## Apologies

| | |
|---|---|
| Excuse me, please. | すみませんがお願いします。<br>[sumimasen ga onegai shi masu] |
| I'm sorry. | ごめんなさい。<br>[gomennasai] |
| I'm really sorry. | 本当にごめんなさい。<br>[hontōni gomennasai] |
| Sorry, it's my fault. | ごめんなさい、私のせいです。<br>[gomennasai, watashi no sei desu] |
| My mistake. | 私の間違いでした。<br>[watashi no machigai deshi ta] |
| May I ...? | …してもいいですか？<br>[… shi te mo ī desu ka ?] |
| Do you mind if I ...? | …してもよろしいですか？<br>[… shi te mo yoroshī desu ka ?] |
| It's OK. | 構いません。<br>[kamai masen] |
| It's all right. | 大丈夫です。<br>[daijōbu desu] |
| Don't worry about it. | それについては心配しないで下さい。<br>[sore ni tuitewa shinpai shi nai<br>de kudasai] |

## Agreement

Yes.　はい。
[hai]

Yes, sure.　はい、もちろん。
[hai, mochiron]

OK (Good!)　わかりました。
[wakari mashi ta]

Very well.　いいですよ。
[ī desuyo]

Certainly!　もちろん！
[mochiron !]

I agree.　賛成です。
[sansei desu]

That's correct.　それは正しい。
[sore wa tadashī]

That's right.　それは正しい。
[sore wa tadashī]

You're right.　あなたは合っています。
[anata wa atte imasu]

I don't mind.　気にしていません。
[kinisite imasen]

Absolutely right.　完全に正しいです。
[kanzen ni tadashī desu]

It's possible.　それは可能です。
[sore wa kanō desu]

That's a good idea.　それはいい考えです。
[sore wa ī kangae desu]

I can't say no.　断ることができません。
[kotowaru koto ga deki masen]

I'd be happy to.　喜んで。
[yorokon de]

With pleasure.　喜んで。
[yorokon de]

## Refusal. Expressing doubt

No.
いいえ。
[īe]

Certainly not.
もちろん、違います。
[mochiron, chigai masu]

I don't agree.
賛成できません。
[sansei deki masen]

I don't think so.
そうは思いません。
[sō wa omoi masen]

It's not true.
それは事実ではありません。
[sore wa jijitsu de wa ari masen]

You are wrong.
あなたは間違っています。
[anata wa machigatte i masu]

I think you are wrong.
あなたは間違っていると思います。
[anata wa machigatte iru to omoi masu]

I'm not sure.
わかりません。
[wakari masen]

It's impossible.
それは不可能です。
[sore wa fukanō desu]

Nothing of the kind (sort)!
まさか！
[masaka !]

The exact opposite.
全く反対です。
[mattaku hantai desu]

I'm against it.
反対です。
[hantai desu]

I don't care.
構いません。
[kamai masen]

I have no idea.
全く分かりません。
[mattaku wakari masen]

I doubt that.
それはどうでしょう。
[sore wa dō desyō]

Sorry, I can't.
申し訳ありませんが、できません。
[mōshiwake arimasenga, deki masen]

Sorry, I don't want to.
申し訳ありませんが、遠慮させて
いただきたいのです。
[mōshiwake arimasenga,ennryosasete
itadakitai no desu]

Thank you, but I don't need this.
ありがとうございます。でもそれは
必要ではありません。
[arigatō gozai masu. demo sore wa
hitsuyō de wa ari masen]

It's late.

もう遅いです。
[mō osoi desu]

I have to get up early.

早く起きなければいけません。
[hayaku oki nakere ba ike masen]

I don't feel well.

気分が悪いのです。
[kibun ga warui nodesu]

## Expressing gratitude

Thank you.　　　　　　　　　　ありがとうございます。
　　　　　　　　　　　　　　　　[arigatō gozai masu]

Thank you very much.　　　　　　どうもありがとうございます。
　　　　　　　　　　　　　　　　[dōmo arigatō gozai masu]

I really appreciate it.　　　　　　本当に感謝しています。
　　　　　　　　　　　　　　　　[hontōni kansha shi te i masu]

I'm really grateful to you.　　　　あなたに本当に感謝しています。
　　　　　　　　　　　　　　　　[anata ni hontōni kansha shi te i masu]

We are really grateful to you.　　私たちはあなたに本当に
　　　　　　　　　　　　　　　　感謝しています。
　　　　　　　　　　　　　　　　[watashi tachi wa anata ni hontōni
　　　　　　　　　　　　　　　　kansha shi te i masu]

Thank you for your time.　　　　お時間を頂きましてありがとう
　　　　　　　　　　　　　　　　ございました。
　　　　　　　　　　　　　　　　[o jikan wo itadaki mashi te arigatō
　　　　　　　　　　　　　　　　gozai mashi ta]

Thanks for everything.　　　　　何もかもありがとうございました。
　　　　　　　　　　　　　　　　[nanimokamo arigatō gozai mashi ta]

Thank you for ...　　　　　　　…をありがとうございます
　　　　　　　　　　　　　　　　[… wo arigatō gozai masu]

your help　　　　　　　　　　助けて頂いて
　　　　　　　　　　　　　　　　[tasuke te itadai te]

a nice time　　　　　　　　　すばらしい時間
　　　　　　　　　　　　　　　　[subarashī jikan]

a wonderful meal　　　　　　素敵なお料理
　　　　　　　　　　　　　　　　[suteki na o ryōri]

a pleasant evening　　　　　楽しい夜
　　　　　　　　　　　　　　　　[tanoshī yoru]

a wonderful day　　　　　　素晴らしい１日
　　　　　　　　　　　　　　　　[subarashī ichinichi]

an amazing journey　　　　楽しい旅
　　　　　　　　　　　　　　　　[tanoshī tabi]

Don't mention it.　　　　　　どういたしまして。
　　　　　　　　　　　　　　　　[dōitashimashite]

You are welcome.　　　　　どういたしまして。
　　　　　　　　　　　　　　　　[dōitashimashite]

Any time.　　　　　　　　いつでもどうぞ。
　　　　　　　　　　　　　　　　[itsu demo dōzo]

My pleasure.　　　　　　どういたしまして。
　　　　　　　　　　　　　　　　[dōitashimashite]

Forget it. It's alright.

忘れて下さい。
[wasure te kudasai]

Don't worry about it.

心配しないで下さい。
[shinpai shi nai de kudasai]

## Congratulations. Best wishes

| | |
|---|---|
| Congratulations! | おめでとうございます！<br>[omedetō gozai masu !] |
| Happy birthday! | お誕生日おめでとうございます！<br>[o tanjō bi omedetō gozai masu !] |
| Merry Christmas! | メリークリスマス！<br>[merīkurisumasu !] |
| Happy New Year! | 新年明けましておめでとう<br>ございます！<br>[shinnen ake mashi te omedetō<br>gozai masu !] |
| Happy Easter! | イースターおめでとうございます！<br>[īsutā omedetō gozai masu !] |
| Happy Hanukkah! | ハヌカおめでとうございます！<br>[hanuka omedetō gozai masu !] |
| I'd like to propose a toast. | 乾杯をあげたいです。<br>[kanpai wo age tai desu] |
| Cheers! | 乾杯！<br>[kanpai !] |
| Let's drink to …! | …のために乾杯しましょう！<br>[… no tame ni kanpai shi masho u !] |
| To our success! | 我々の成功のために！<br>[wareware no seikō no tame ni !] |
| To your success! | あなたの成功のために！<br>[anata no seikō no tame ni !] |
| Good luck! | 幸運を祈るよ！<br>[kōun wo inoru yo !] |
| Have a nice day! | 良い一日をお過ごし下さい！<br>[yoi ichi nichi wo osugoshi kudasai !] |
| Have a good holiday! | 良い休日をお過ごし下さい！<br>[yoi kyūjitsu wo osugoshi kudasai !] |
| Have a safe journey! | 道中ご無事で！<br>[dōtyū gobujide!] |
| I hope you get better soon! | 早く良くなるといいですね！<br>[hayaku yoku naru to ī desu ne !] |

## Socializing

| | |
|---|---|
| Why are you sad? | なぜ悲しいのですか？<br>[naze kanashī no desu ka ?] |
| Smile! Cheer up! | 笑って！　元気を出してください！<br>[waratte ! genki wo dashite kudasai !] |
| Are you free tonight? | 今夜あいていますか？<br>[konya ai te i masu ka ?] |
| May I offer you a drink? | 何か飲みますか？<br>[nani ka nomi masu ka ?] |
| Would you like to dance? | 踊りませんか？<br>[odori masen ka ?] |
| Let's go to the movies. | 映画に行きましょう。<br>[eiga ni iki masho u] |
| May I invite you to …? | …へ誘ってもいいですか？<br>[… e sasotte mo ī desu ka ?] |
| a restaurant | レストラン<br>[resutoran] |
| the movies | 映画<br>[eiga] |
| the theater | 劇場<br>[gekijō] |
| go for a walk | 散歩<br>[sanpo] |
| At what time? | 何時に？<br>[nan ji ni ?] |
| tonight | 今晩<br>[konban] |
| at six | 6時<br>[roku ji] |
| at seven | 7時<br>[shichi ji] |
| at eight | 8時<br>[hachi ji] |
| at nine | 9時<br>[kyū ji] |
| Do you like it here? | ここが好きですか？<br>[koko ga suki desu ka ?] |
| Are you here with someone? | ここで誰かと一緒ですか？<br>[koko de dare ka to issyodesu ka ?] |
| I'm with my friend. | 友達と一緒です。<br>[tomodachi to issho desu] |

| | |
|---|---|
| I'm with my friends. | 友人たちと一緒です。<br>[yūjin tachi to issho desu] |
| No, I'm alone. | いいえ、一人です。<br>[īe, hitori desu] |

| | |
|---|---|
| Do you have a boyfriend? | 彼氏いるの？<br>[kareshi iru no ?] |
| I have a boyfriend. | 私は彼氏がいます。<br>[watashi wa kareshi ga i masu] |
| Do you have a girlfriend? | 彼女いるの？<br>[kanojo iru no ?] |
| I have a girlfriend. | 私は彼女がいます。<br>[watashi wa kanojo ga i masu] |

| | |
|---|---|
| Can I see you again? | また会えるかな？<br>[mata aeru ka na ?] |
| Can I call you? | 電話してもいい？<br>[denwa shi te mo ī ?] |
| Call me. (Give me a call.) | 電話してね。<br>[denwa shi te ne] |
| What's your number? | 電話番号は？<br>[denwa bangō wa ?] |
| I miss you. | 寂しくなるよ。<br>[sabishiku naru yo] |

| | |
|---|---|
| You have a beautiful name. | 綺麗なお名前ですね。<br>[kirei na o namae desu ne] |
| I love you. | 愛しているよ。<br>[aishi te iru yo] |
| Will you marry me? | 結婚しようか<br>[kekkon shiyo u ka] |
| You're kidding! | 冗談でしょう！<br>[jōdan dessyō!] |
| I'm just kidding. | 冗談だよ。<br>[jōdan da yo] |

| | |
|---|---|
| Are you serious? | 本気ですか？<br>[honki desuka ?] |
| I'm serious. | 本気です。<br>[honki desu] |
| Really?! | 本当ですか？！<br>[hontō desu ka ?!] |
| It's unbelievable! | 信じられません！<br>[shinjirare masen !] |
| I don't believe you. | あなたは信じられません。<br>[anata wa shinjirare masen] |
| I can't. | 私にはできません。<br>[watashi ni wa deki masen] |
| I don't know. | わかりません。<br>[wakari masen] |
| I don't understand you. | おっしゃることが分かりません。<br>[ossharu koto ga wakari masen] |

Please go away.　　　　　　　出ていって下さい。
　　　　　　　　　　　　　　[de te itte kudasai]

Leave me alone!　　　　　　ほっといて下さい！
　　　　　　　　　　　　　　[hottoi te kudasai !]

I can't stand him.　　　　　彼には耐えられない。
　　　　　　　　　　　　　　[kare ni wa taerare nai]

You are disgusting!　　　　いやな人ですね！
　　　　　　　　　　　　　　[iyana hito desu ne !]

I'll call the police!　　　　警察を呼びますよ！
　　　　　　　　　　　　　　[keisatsu wo yobi masuyo !]

## Sharing impressions. Emotions

I like it.
これが好きです。
[kore ga suki desu]

Very nice.
とても素晴らしい。
[totemo subarashī]

That's great!
それはすばらしいです！
[sore wa subarashī desu !]

It's not bad.
それは悪くはないです。
[sore wa waruku wa nai desu]

I don't like it.
それが好きではありません。
[sore ga suki de wa ari masen]

It's not good.
それはよくないです。
[sore wa yoku nai desu]

It's bad.
それはひどいです。
[sore wa hidoi desu]

It's very bad.
それはとてもひどいです。
[sore wa totemo hidoi desu]

It's disgusting.
それは最悪です。
[sore wa saiaku desu]

I'm happy.
幸せです。
[shiawase desu]

I'm content.
満足しています。
[manzoku shi te i masu]

I'm in love.
好きな人がいます。
[suki na hito ga i masu]

I'm calm.
冷静です。
[reisei desu]

I'm bored.
退屈です。
[taikutsu desu]

I'm tired.
疲れています。
[tsukare te i masu]

I'm sad.
悲しいです。
[kanashī desu]

I'm frightened.
怖いです。
[kowai desu]

I'm angry.
腹が立ちます。
[haraga tachi masu]

I'm worried.
心配しています。
[shinpai shi te i masu]

I'm nervous.
緊張しています。
[kinchō shi te i masu]

I'm jealous. (envious)　　　　　　　嫉妬しています。
　　　　　　　　　　　　　　　　[shitto shi te i masu]

I'm surprised.　　　　　　　　　　驚いています。
　　　　　　　　　　　　　　　　[odoroi te i masu]

I'm perplexed.　　　　　　　　　　恥ずかしいです。
　　　　　　　　　　　　　　　　[hazukashī desu]

## Problems. Accidents

I've got a problem. 困っています。
[komatte imasu]

We've got a problem. 困っています。
[komatte imasu]

I'm lost. 道に迷いました。
[michi ni mayoi mashi ta]

I missed the last bus (train). 最終バス（電車）を逃しました。
[saishūbasu (densha) wo nogashi mashi ta]

I don't have any money left. もうお金がありません。
[mō okane ga ari masen]

I've lost my … …を失くしました
[… wo nakushi mashi ta]

Someone stole my … …を盗まれました
[… wo nusumare mashi ta]

passport パスポート
[pasupōto]

wallet 財布
[saifu]

papers 書類
[shorui]

ticket 切符
[kippu]

money お金
[okane]

handbag ハンドバック
[handobakku]

camera カメラ
[kamera]

laptop ノートパソコン
[nōto pasokon]

tablet computer タブレット型コンピューター
[taburetto gata konpyūtā]

mobile phone 携帯電話
[keitai denwa]

Help me! 助けて下さい！
[tasuke te kudasai !]

What's happened? どうしましたか？
[dō shi mashi ta ka ?]

fire

火災
[kasai]

shooting

発砲
[happō]

murder

殺人
[satsujin]

explosion

爆発
[bakuhatsu]

fight

けんか
[kenka]

Call the police!

警察を呼んで下さい！
[keisatsu wo yon de kudasai !]

Please hurry up!

急いで下さい！
[isoi de kudasai !]

I'm looking for the police station.

警察署を探しています。
[keisatsu sho wo sagashi te imasu]

I need to make a call.

電話をしなければなりません。
[denwa wo shi nakere ba nari masen]

May I use your phone?

お電話をお借りしても良いですか？
[o denwa wo o karishi te mo ī desu ka ?]

I've been ...

…されました
[… sare mashi ta]

mugged

強盗
[gōtō]

robbed

盗まれる
[nusumareru]

raped

レイプ
[reipu]

attacked (beaten up)

暴行される
[bōkō sareru]

Are you all right?

大丈夫ですか？
[daijōbu desu ka ?]

Did you see who it was?

誰が犯人か見ましたか？
[dare ga hanninn ka mi mashi ta ka ?]

Would you be able to recognize the person?

その人がどんな人か
分かりますか？
[sono hito ga donna hito ka
wakari masu ka?]

Are you sure?

本当に大丈夫ですか？
[hontōni daijōbu desu ka ?]

Please calm down.

落ち着いて下さい。
[ochitsui te kudasai]

Take it easy!

気楽に！
[kiraku ni !]

Don't worry!

心配しないで！
[shinpai shi nai de !]

Everything will be fine.

大丈夫ですから。
[daijōbu desu kara]

Everything's all right.

大丈夫ですから。
[daijōbu desu kara]

Come here, please.

こちらに来て下さい。
[kochira ni ki te kudasai]

I have some questions for you.

いくつかお伺いしたいことがあります。
[ikutuka o ukagai shi tai koto ga ari masu]

Wait a moment, please.

少しお待ち下さい。
[sukoshi omachi kudasai]

Do you have any I.D.?

身分証明書はお持ちですか？
[mibun shōmei sho wa o mochi desu ka ?]

Thanks. You can leave now.

ありがとうございます。もう
行っていいですよ。
[arigatō gozai masu. mō
itte ī desuyo]

Hands behind your head!

両手を頭の後ろで組みなさい！
[ryōute wo atama
no ushiro de kuminasai !]

You're under arrest!

逮捕します
[taiho shi masu]

## Health problems

| | |
|---|---|
| Please help me. | 助けて下さい。<br>[tasuke te kudasai] |
| I don't feel well. | 気分が悪いのです。<br>[kibun ga warui nodesu] |
| My husband doesn't feel well. | 主人の具合が悪いのです。<br>[shujin no guai ga warui no desu] |
| My son ... | 息子の…<br>[musuko no …] |
| My father ... | 父の…<br>[chichi no …] |
| My wife doesn't feel well. | 妻の具合が悪いのです。<br>[tsuma no guai ga warui no desu] |
| My daughter ... | 娘の…<br>[musume no …] |
| My mother ... | 母の…<br>[haha no …] |
| I've got a ... | …がします<br>[… ga shi masu] |
| headache | 頭痛<br>[zutsū] |
| sore throat | 喉が痛い<br>[nodo ga itai] |
| stomach ache | 腹痛<br>[fukutsū] |
| toothache | 歯痛<br>[shitsū] |
| I feel dizzy. | めまいがします。<br>[memai ga shi masu] |
| He has a fever. | 彼は熱があります。<br>[kare wa netsu ga ari masu] |
| She has a fever. | 彼女は熱があります。<br>[kanojo wa netsu ga ari masu] |
| I can't breathe. | 息ができません。<br>[iki ga deki masen] |
| I'm short of breath. | 息切れがします。<br>[ikigire ga shi masu] |
| I am asthmatic. | 喘息です。<br>[zensoku desu] |
| I am diabetic. | 糖尿病です。<br>[tōnyō byō desu] |

I can't sleep.

不眠症です。
[huminsyō desu]

food poisoning

食中毒
[shokuchūdoku]

---

It hurts here.

ここが痛いです。
[koko ga itai desu]

Help me!

助けて下さい！
[tasuke te kudasai !]

I am here!

ここにいます！
[koko ni i masu !]

We are here!

私たちはここにいます！
[watashi tachi wa koko ni i masu !]

Get me out of here!

ここから出して下さい！
[koko kara dashi te kudasai !]

I need a doctor.

医者に診せる必要があります。
[isha ni miseru hituyō ga arimasu]

I can't move.

動けません！
[ugoke masen !]

I can't move my legs.

足が動きません。
[ashi ga ugoki masen]

---

I have a wound.

傷があります。
[kizu ga ari masu]

Is it serious?

それは重傷ですか？
[sore wa jūsyō desu ka ?]

My documents are in my pocket.

私に関する書類はポケッ
トに入っています。
[watashi nikansuru shorui wa poketto
ni haitte i masu]

Calm down!

落ち着いて下さい！
[ochitsui te kudasai !]

May I use your phone?

お電話をお借りしても良いですか？
[o denwa wo o karishi te mo ī desu ka ?]

---

Call an ambulance!

救急車を呼んで下さい！
[kyūkyū sha wo yon de kudasai !]

It's urgent!

緊急です！
[kinkyū desu !]

It's an emergency!

緊急です！
[kinkyū desu !]

Please hurry up!

急いで下さい！
[isoi de kudasai !]

Would you please call a doctor?

医者を呼んでいただけますか？
[isha wo yon de itadake masu ka ?]

Where is the hospital?

病院はどこですか？
[byōin wa doko desu ka ?]

---

How are you feeling?

ご気分はいかがですか？
[gokibun wa ikaga desu ka ?]

Are you all right?

大丈夫ですか？
[daijōbu desu ka ?]

What's happened?

どうしましたか？
[dō shi mashi ta ka ?]

I feel better now.

もう気分が良くなりました。
[mō kibun ga yoku narimashita]

It's OK.

大丈夫です。
[daijōbu desu]

It's all right.

大丈夫です。
[daijōbu desu]

## At the pharmacy

| | |
|---|---|
| pharmacy (drugstore) | 薬局<br>[yakkyoku] |
| 24-hour pharmacy | ２４時間営業の薬局<br>[nijyū yo jikan eigyō no yakkyoku] |
| Where is the closest pharmacy? | 一番近くの薬局はどこですか？<br>[ichiban chikaku no yakkyoku wa doko desu ka?] |
| Is it open now? | 今開いていますか？<br>[ima ai te i masu ka ?] |
| At what time does it open? | 何時に開きますか？<br>[nan ji ni aki masu ka ?] |
| At what time does it close? | 何時に閉まりますか？<br>[nan ji ni shimari masu ka ?] |
| Is it far? | 遠いですか？<br>[tōi desu ka ?] |
| Can I get there on foot? | そこまで歩いて行けますか？<br>[soko made arui te ike masu ka ?] |
| Can you show me on the map? | 地図で教えて頂けますか？<br>[chizu de oshie te itadake masu ka ?] |
| Please give me something for ... | 何か…に効くものを下さい<br>[nani ka ... ni kiku mono wo kudasai] |
| a headache | 頭痛<br>[zutsū] |
| a cough | 咳<br>[seki] |
| a cold | 風邪<br>[kaze] |
| the flu | インフルエンザ<br>[infuruenza] |
| a fever | 発熱<br>[hatsunetsu] |
| a stomach ache | 胃痛<br>[itsū] |
| nausea | 吐き気<br>[hakike] |
| diarrhea | 下痢<br>[geri] |
| constipation | 便秘<br>[benpi] |

| | |
|---|---|
| pain in the back | 腰痛<br>[yōtsū] |
| chest pain | 胸痛<br>[kyōtsū] |
| side stitch | 脇腹の痛み<br>[wakibara no itami] |
| abdominal pain | 腹痛<br>[fukutsū] |

| | |
|---|---|
| pill | 薬<br>[kusuri] |
| ointment, cream | 軟膏、クリーム<br>[nankō, kurīmu] |
| syrup | シロップ<br>[shiroppu] |
| spray | スプレー<br>[supurē] |
| drops | 目薬<br>[megusuri] |

| | |
|---|---|
| You need to go to the hospital. | 病院に行かなくてはなりません。<br>[byōin ni ika naku te wa nari masen] |
| health insurance | 健康保険<br>[kenkō hoken] |
| prescription | 処方箋<br>[shohōsen] |
| insect repellant | 虫除け<br>[mushiyoke] |
| Band Aid | 絆創膏<br>[bansōkō] |

## The bare minimum

Excuse me, …
すみません、…
[sumimasen, …]

Hello.
こんにちは。
[konnichiwa]

Thank you.
ありがとうございます。
[arigatō gozai masu]

Good bye.
さようなら。
[sayōnara]

Yes.
はい。
[hai]

No.
いいえ。
[īe]

I don't know.
わかりません。
[wakari masen]

Where? | Where to? | When?
どこ？ | どこへ？ | いつ？
[doko ? | doko e ? | i tsu ?]

I need …
…が必要です
[… ga hitsuyō desu]

I want …
したいです
[shi tai desu]

Do you have …?
…をお持ちですか？
[… wo o mochi desu ka ?]

Is there a … here?
ここには…がありますか？
[koko ni wa … ga ari masu ka ?]

May I …?
…してもいいですか？
[… shi te mo ī desu ka ?]

…, please (polite request)
お願いします。
[onegai shi masu]

I'm looking for …
…を探しています
[… wo sagashi te i masu]

restroom
トイレ
[toire]

ATM
ＡＴＭ
[ētīemu]

pharmacy (drugstore)
薬局
[yakkyoku]

hospital
病院
[byōin]

police station
警察
[keisatsu]

subway
地下鉄
[chikatetsu]

| | |
|---|---|
| taxi | タクシー<br>[takushī] |
| train station | 駅<br>[eki] |

| | |
|---|---|
| My name is ... | 私は…と申します<br>[watashi wa ... to mōshi masu] |
| What's your name? | お名前は何ですか？<br>[o namae wa nan desu ka ?] |
| Could you please help me? | 助けていただけますか？<br>[tasuke te itadake masu ka ?] |
| I've got a problem. | 困ったことがあります。<br>[komatta koto ga arimasu] |
| I don't feel well. | 気分が悪いのです。<br>[kibun ga warui nodesu] |
| Call an ambulance! | 救急車を呼んで下さい！<br>[kyūkyū sha wo yon de kudasai !] |
| May I make a call? | 電話をしてもいいですか？<br>[denwa wo shi te mo ī desu ka ?] |

| | |
|---|---|
| I'm sorry. | ごめんなさい。<br>[gomennasai] |
| You're welcome. | どういたしまして。<br>[dōitashimashite] |

| | |
|---|---|
| I, me | 私<br>[watashi] |
| you (inform.) | 君<br>[kimi] |
| he | 彼<br>[kare] |
| she | 彼女<br>[kanojo] |
| they (masc.) | 彼ら<br>[karera] |
| they (fem.) | 彼女たち<br>[kanojotachi] |
| we | 私たち<br>[watashi tachi] |
| you (pl) | 君たち<br>[kimi tachi] |
| you (sg, form.) | あなた<br>[anata] |

| | |
|---|---|
| ENTRANCE | 入り口<br>[iriguchi] |
| EXIT | 出口<br>[deguchi] |
| OUT OF ORDER | 故障中<br>[koshō chū] |
| CLOSED | 休業中<br>[kyūgyō chū] |

| OPEN | 営業中 |
| | [eigyō chū] |
| FOR WOMEN | 女性用 |
| | [josei yō] |
| FOR MEN | 男性用 |
| | [dansei yō] |

# MINI DICTIONARY

This section contains 250
useful words required for
everyday communication.
You will find the names of
months and days of the week
here. The dictionary also
contains topics such as colors,
measurements, family, and
more

T&P Books Publishing

# DICTIONARY CONTENTS

T&P Books Publishing

## 1. Time. Calendar

| | | |
|---|---|---|
| time | 時間 | jikan |
| hour | 時間 | jikan |
| half an hour | ３０分 | san jū fun |
| minute | 分 | fun, pun |
| second | 秒 | byō |
| | | |
| today (adv) | 今日 | kyō |
| tomorrow (adv) | 明日 | ashita |
| yesterday (adv) | 昨日 | kinō |
| | | |
| Monday | 月曜日 | getsuyōbi |
| Tuesday | 火曜日 | kayōbi |
| Wednesday | 水曜日 | suiyōbi |
| Thursday | 木曜日 | mokuyōbi |
| Friday | 金曜日 | kinyōbi |
| Saturday | 土曜日 | doyōbi |
| Sunday | 日曜日 | nichiyōbi |
| | | |
| day | 日 | nichi |
| working day | 営業日 | eigyōbi |
| public holiday | 公休 | kōkyū |
| weekend | 週末 | shūmatsu |
| | | |
| week | 週 | shū |
| last week (adv) | 先週 | senshū |
| next week (adv) | 来週 | raishū |
| | | |
| in the morning | 朝に | asa ni |
| in the afternoon | 午後に | gogo ni |
| | | |
| in the evening | 夕方に | yūgata ni |
| tonight (this evening) | 今夜 | konya |
| | | |
| at night | 夜に | yoru ni |
| midnight | 真夜中 | mayonaka |
| | | |
| January | 一月 | ichigatsu |
| February | 二月 | nigatsu |
| March | 三月 | sangatsu |
| April | 四月 | shigatsu |
| May | 五月 | gogatsu |
| June | 六月 | rokugatsu |
| | | |
| July | 七月 | shichigatsu |
| August | 八月 | hachigatsu |

| September | 九月 | kugatsu |
|---|---|---|
| October | 十月 | jūgatsu |
| November | 十一月 | jūichigatsu |
| December | 十二月 | jūnigatsu |

| in spring | 春に | haru ni |
|---|---|---|
| in summer | 夏に | natsu ni |
| in fall | 秋に | aki ni |
| in winter | 冬に | fuyu ni |

| month | 月 | tsuki |
|---|---|---|
| season (summer, etc.) | 季節 | kisetsu |
| year | 年 | nen |

## 2. Numbers. Numerals

| 0 zero | ゼロ | zero |
|---|---|---|
| 1 one | 一 | ichi |
| 2 two | 二 | ni |
| 3 three | 三 | san |
| 4 four | 四 | yon |

| 5 five | 五 | go |
|---|---|---|
| 6 six | 六 | roku |
| 7 seven | 七 | nana |
| 8 eight | 八 | hachi |
| 9 nine | 九 | kyū |
| 10 ten | 十 | jū |

| 11 eleven | 十一 | jū ichi |
|---|---|---|
| 12 twelve | 十二 | jū ni |
| 13 thirteen | 十三 | jū san |
| 14 fourteen | 十四 | jū yon |
| 15 fifteen | 十五 | jū go |

| 16 sixteen | 十六 | jū roku |
|---|---|---|
| 17 seventeen | 十七 | jū shichi |
| 18 eighteen | 十八 | jū hachi |
| 19 nineteen | 十九 | jū kyū |

| 20 twenty | 二十 | ni jū |
|---|---|---|
| 30 thirty | 三十 | san jū |
| 40 forty | 四十 | yon jū |
| 50 fifty | 五十 | go jū |

| 60 sixty | 六十 | roku jū |
|---|---|---|
| 70 seventy | 七十 | nana jū |
| 80 eighty | 八十 | hachi jū |
| 90 ninety | 九十 | kyū jū |
| 100 one hundred | 百 | hyaku |

| | | |
|---|---|---|
| 200 two hundred | 二百 | ni hyaku |
| 300 three hundred | 三百 | san byaku |
| 400 four hundred | 四百 | yon hyaku |
| 500 five hundred | 五百 | go hyaku |
| 600 six hundred | 六百 | roppyaku |
| 700 seven hundred | 七百 | nana hyaku |
| 800 eight hundred | 八百 | happyaku |
| 900 nine hundred | 九百 | kyū hyaku |
| 1000 one thousand | 千 | sen |
| 10000 ten thousand | 一万 | ichiman |
| one hundred thousand | １０万 | jyūman |
| million | 百万 | hyakuman |
| billion | 十億 | jūoku |

## 3. Humans. Family

| | | |
|---|---|---|
| man (adult male) | 男性 | dansei |
| young man | 若者 | wakamono |
| woman | 女性 | josei |
| girl (young woman) | 少女 | shōjo |
| old man | 老人 | rōjin |
| old woman | 老婦人 | rō fujin |
| mother | 母親 | hahaoya |
| father | 父親 | chichioya |
| son | 息子 | musuko |
| daughter | 娘 | musume |
| brother | 兄、弟、兄弟 | ani, otōto, kyoōdai |
| sister | 姉、妹、姉妹 | ane, imōto, shimai |
| parents | 親 | oya |
| child | 子供 | kodomo |
| children | 子供 | kodomo |
| stepmother | 継母 | keibo |
| stepfather | 継父 | keifu |
| grandmother | 祖母 | sobo |
| grandfather | 祖父 | sofu |
| grandson | 孫息子 | mago musuko |
| granddaughter | 孫娘 | mago musume |
| grandchildren | 孫 | mago |
| uncle | 伯父 | oji |
| aunt | 伯母 | oba |
| nephew | 甥 | oi |
| niece | 姪 | mei |
| wife | 妻 | tsuma |

| | | |
|---|---|---|
| husband | 夫 | otto |
| married (masc.) | 既婚の | kikon no |
| married (fem.) | 既婚の | kikon no |
| widow | 未亡人 | mibōjin |
| widower | 男やもめ | otokoyamome |
| | | |
| name (first name) | 名前 | namae |
| surname (last name) | 姓 | sei |
| | | |
| relative | 親戚 | shinseki |
| friend (masc.) | 友達 | tomodachi |
| friendship | 友情 | yūjō |
| | | |
| partner | パートナー | pātonā |
| superior (n) | 上司、上役 | jōshi, uwayaku |
| colleague | 同僚 | dōryō |
| neighbors | 隣人 | rinjin |

## 4. Human body

| | | |
|---|---|---|
| body | 身体 | shintai |
| heart | 心臓 | shinzō |
| blood | 血液 | ketsueki |
| brain | 脳 | nō |
| | | |
| bone | 骨 | hone |
| spine (backbone) | 背骨 | sebone |
| rib | 肋骨 | rokkotsu |
| lungs | 肺 | hai |
| skin | 肌 | hada |
| | | |
| head | 頭 | atama |
| face | 顔 | kao |
| nose | 鼻 | hana |
| forehead | 額 | hitai |
| cheek | 頬 | hō |
| | | |
| mouth | 口 | kuchi |
| tongue | 舌 | shita |
| tooth | 歯 | ha |
| lips | 唇 | kuchibiru |
| chin | あご（頤） | ago |
| | | |
| ear | 耳 | mimi |
| neck | 首 | kubi |
| eye | 眼 | me |
| pupil | 瞳 | hitomi |
| eyebrow | 眉 | mayu |
| eyelash | まつげ | matsuge |
| hair | 髪の毛 | kaminoke |

| hairstyle | 髪形 | kamigata |
| mustache | 口ひげ | kuchihige |
| beard | あごひげ | agohige |
| to have (a beard, etc.) | 生やしている | hayashi te iru |
| bald (adj) | はげ頭の | hageatama no |

| hand | 手 | te |
| arm | 腕 | ude |
| finger | 指 | yubi |
| nail | 爪 | tsume |
| palm | 手のひら | tenohira |

| shoulder | 肩 | kata |
| leg | 足 [脚] | ashi |
| knee | 膝 | hiza |
| heel | かかと [踵] | kakato |
| back | 背中 | senaka |

## 5. Clothing. Personal accessories

| clothes | 洋服 | yōfuku |
| coat (overcoat) | オーバーコート | ōbā kōto |
| fur coat | 毛皮のコート | kegawa no kōto |
| jacket (e.g., leather ~) | ジャケット | jaketto |
| raincoat (trenchcoat, etc.) | レインコート | reinkōto |

| shirt (button shirt) | ワイシャツ | waishatsu |
| pants | ズボン | zubon |
| suit jacket | ジャケット | jaketto |
| suit | 背広 | sebiro |

| dress (frock) | ドレス | doresu |
| skirt | スカート | sukāto |
| T-shirt | Tシャツ | tīshatsu |
| bathrobe | バスローブ | basurōbu |
| pajamas | パジャマ | pajama |
| workwear | 作業服 | sagyō fuku |

| underwear | 下着 | shitagi |
| socks | 靴下 | kutsushita |
| bra | ブラジャー | burajā |
| pantyhose | パンティストッキング | pantī sutokkingu |
| stockings (thigh highs) | ストッキング | sutokkingu |
| bathing suit | 水着 | mizugi |

| hat | 帽子 | bōshi |
| footwear | 靴 | kutsu |
| boots (cowboy ~) | ブーツ | būtsu |
| heel | かかと [踵] | kakato |
| shoestring | 靴ひも | kutsu himo |

| shoe polish | 靴クリーム | kutsu kurīmu |
| gloves | 手袋 | tebukuro |
| mittens | ミトン | miton |
| scarf (muffler) | マフラー | mafurā |
| glasses (eyeglasses) | めがね [眼鏡] | megane |
| umbrella | 傘 | kasa |

| tie (necktie) | ネクタイ | nekutai |
| handkerchief | ハンカチ | hankachi |
| comb | くし [櫛] | kushi |
| hairbrush | ヘアブラシ | hea burashi |

| buckle | バックル | bakkuru |
| belt | ベルト | beruto |
| purse | ハンドバッグ | hando baggu |

## 6. House. Apartment

| apartment | アパート | apāto |
| room | 部屋 | heya |
| bedroom | 寝室 | shinshitsu |
| dining room | 食堂 | shokudō |

| living room | 居間 | ima |
| study (home office) | 書斎 | shosai |
| entry room | 玄関 | genkan |
| bathroom (room with a bath or shower) | 浴室 | yokushitsu |
| half bath | トイレ | toire |

| vacuum cleaner | 掃除機 | sōji ki |
| mop | モップ | moppu |
| dust cloth | ダストクロス | dasuto kurosu |
| short broom | ほうき | hōki |
| dustpan | ちりとり | chiritori |

| furniture | 家具 | kagu |
| table | テーブル | tēburu |
| chair | 椅子 | isu |
| armchair | 肘掛け椅子 | hijikake isu |

| mirror | 鏡 | kagami |
| carpet | カーペット | kāpetto |
| fireplace | 暖炉 | danro |
| drapes | カーテン | kāten |
| table lamp | テーブルランプ | tēburu ranpu |
| chandelier | シャンデリア | shanderia |

| kitchen | 台所 | daidokoro |
| gas stove (range) | ガスコンロ | gasu konro |

| electric stove | 電気コンロ | denki konro |
| microwave oven | 電子レンジ | denshi renji |

| refrigerator | 冷蔵庫 | reizōko |
| freezer | 冷凍庫 | reitōko |
| dishwasher | 食器洗い機 | shokkiarai ki |
| faucet | 蛇口 | jaguchi |

| meat grinder | 肉挽き器 | niku hiki ki |
| juicer | ジューサー | jūsā |
| toaster | トースター | tōsutā |
| mixer | ハンドミキサー | hando mikisā |

| coffee machine | コーヒーメーカー | kōhī mēkā |
| kettle | やかん | yakan |
| teapot | 急須 | kyūsu |

| TV set | テレビ | terebi |
| VCR (video recorder) | ビデオ | bideo |
| iron (e.g., steam ~) | アイロン | airon |
| telephone | 電話 | denwa |